Asik Rahaman Jamader
Mohammad Israr
Anupama Das

Healthcare & Hospitality Management : An Innovative Approach

Asik Rahaman Jamader
Mohammad Israr
Anupama Das

Healthcare & Hospitality Management : An Innovative Approach

An Innovative Approach

Noor Publishing

Imprint

Any brand names and product names mentioned in this book are subject to trademark, brand or patent protection and are trademarks or registered trademarks of their respective holders. The use of brand names, product names, common names, trade names, product descriptions etc. even without a particular marking in this work is in no way to be construed to mean that such names may be regarded as unrestricted in respect of trademark and brand protection legislation and could thus be used by anyone.

Cover image: www.ingimage.com

Publisher:
Noor Publishing
is a trademark of
Dodo Books Indian Ocean Ltd., member of the OmniScriptum S.R.L Publishing group
str. A.Russo 15, of. 61, Chisinau-2068, Republic of Moldova Europe
Printed at: see last page
ISBN: 978-620-3-86031-3

Healthcare & Hospitality Management: An Innovative Approach

By

Asik Rahaman Jamader
Lecturer,
Department Of Tourism & Hotel Management
Penguin School of Hotel Management, Kolkata, India

Prof. (Dr.) Mohammad Israr
Department of Mechanical Engineering
Poornima College of Engineering, Jaipur, Rajasthan, India

Anupama Das
Department of Optometry
NSHM Knowledge Campus Kolkata, India

Table of Contents

Abstract... 5

Chapter 1: About health care management 6

   Health care management and Its History: 6

   The role of administration in the health system: 6

   Managed care organizations roles and the future of health insurance: 7

   The role of administration in health systems: 8

   The role of administration in health systems: 8

   The major two projects that were approved and implemented were: 8

   Some of the benefits of my-CARE-Cerner ADT Interface: 9

Chapter 2: About Hospitality Management 11

   Hospitality & its History: 11

   Size and Scope of the Sector: 14

   Productivity: 14

   Workforce: 14

   Core Occupation: 15

   Key occupations: 15

   Hard to fill vacancies and skill shortages: 15

   Labor Turnover: 15

   Skills Gaps: 15

   Training and Development: 16

   Industries Covered: 16

   Membership Clubs: 16

   British Hospitality Association: 16

   Restaurant Staffing and Structures: 17

   Current Eating Trends: 20

   Eating Away from Home: 20

   Dieting: 20

   Supplements: 21

   Convenience Foods: 21

Ethnic Foods: 21

Functional Foods: 21

Chapter 3: Health care management and its importance 22

What does healthcare management involve? 23

What does a healthcare manager do? 23

Why is healthcare management important? 23

Healthcare industry growth: 24

Chapter 4: Hospitality Management and its Importance. 25

The Importance of Outstanding Hospitality Management: 25

Chapter 5: Innovative Implementation in the Health Care Management. 27

Manager's Responsibilities: 28

Implementing Innovative Practices: 28

Chapter 6: Innovative Implementations in Hospitality Management. 30

Organizational Teams: 30

Knowledge Management and Sharing: 31

Team Culture: 31

Managerial Implications: 32

Chapter 7: Artificial intelligence in health care and hospitality 33

Intelligence in hospitality: 33

In-Person Customer Service: 34

Chat bots and Messaging: 34

Data Analysis: 34

More Digital Trends: 34

Artificial Intelligence in healthcare: 35

Human Intelligence in Decision Making: 35

Artificial Intelligence in Robotics: 35

Artificial Intelligence in Healthcare: 36

Chapter 8: New Innovation on Healthcare and Hospitality 37

AI stands for artificial intelligence: 37

Mayo Clinic and Google Take Relationship to Next Level: 37

5 Lessons Learned While Launching a Virtual ICU during the Pandemic: 37

How Collaboration Accelerates Innovation during the Pandemic 38

Tele health TVs' Position Intermountain for the Future of Virtual Care: 38

5 Ways Virtual Reality Can Better Prepare Future Surgeons: 39

New Innovation on Hospitality Management: 39

In The Hotel, There Are Five Factors That Influence Innovation. 40

Market Factor and Competition 40

Provide Value To A Customer's Stay At A Hotel, As Listed Below: 41

Food and Beverage-Related Service: 41

Hospitality Trends (Eco-Friendly Initiatives): 42

Hotels with a Personal Touch:' 43

Spa Energy: 43

There aren't any pet-friendly initiatives: 43

Traditional Wines are making a Comeback: 43

Eco-Friendly Hospitality Initiatives 43

Hotels That Are Environmentally Friendly Are In Tune With Nature: 44

'Green' Hotels That Rule The Roost Benefit The Environment In The Following Ways: 44

Eco-Friendly Lodging Helps To Reduce Material Use. 44

A Proactive Environmental Strategy Should Be Implemented By An Eco Hotel: 44

Luxury and accommodation comfort are not sacrificed in an eco-friendly hotel: 45

Chapter 9: Economic Growth in Healthcare 46

What Impact Does Health Care Have on the Economy? 46

The Economic Impact on Health Care 47

Chapter 10: Economic growth in hospitality 48

The Following Industries May Be Included In The Hospitality Industry: 49

As A Market Category, Marriot Runs and Owns A Luxury Hotel Group: 49

The Hospitality Sector (Hotels And Restaurants) Is Critical To The Industry's Success: 50

Hotels and Hospitality: 50

Employment and Hospitality: 50

Industrial sector of leisure and Hospitality: 51

Reference: 52

Abstract

A variety of things must be considered by organizations wanting to develop creative settings in health care. These include making sufficient resources available, such as money and physical space, but also coordination and consultation regarding intellectual property and licensing; facilitating access to engineers, software developers, and behavioral scientists; making providers and patients available to innovators; maintaining a sufficiently long-term perspective; and isolating the innovation group from operational demands. This paper looks at best practices, success factors, and problems in the development of strategic innovation in the hotel industry in general, as well as in the sales, marketing, and revenue management divisions in particular. Despite a growing understanding of the necessity of formal innovation processes in the hospitality sector, many businesses are still seen as non-innovative. Three major conclusions are presented in the paper.

Chapter 1: About health care management

Health care management and Its History:

There are a variety of reasons why health care is such an essential part of our everyday lives. Dieticians, nurses, physicians, dieticians, and therapists are all part of healthcare, which many people are unaware of. They all tend to play a significant part in ensuring that everyone, whether American or from another nation, maintains their health. "Sometimes, an ounce of prevention is worth more than an ounce of treatment". Even though many people feel these tasks are simple, I believe they are not simple and need a great deal of hard work, attention, and time to ensure that everyone is well taken care of. The function of health care administrators in various situations, the future of health insurance, the role of administration in health systems, and the role of managed care organizations will all be discussed in this article.

The role of administration in the health system:

Because of the vast range of contexts in which health care managers might work, they can play a number of responsibilities. I now work as a Senior Buyer in the Materials Management Department for Catholic Healthcare West (CHW), a Health Care Organization (HCO), at St. Joseph's Hospital and Medical Center (SJHMC) in Phoenix, AZ. With 60,000 physicians, clinicians, and non-clinical support personnel, CHW is a Catholic non-profit public healthcare organization with over forty networks of clinics and hospitals offering medical services in Arizona, California, and Nevada. CHW employs health care administrators at various levels, including top, medium, and entry.

SJHMC has two medical management committees: the Critical Care Committee and the Risk Management Committee, both of which play an important part in the administration of their health care system. The critical care committee assesses the critical care practice standards for the hospital's different intensive care and emergency units. Through the continuing and concentrated monitoring of important quality indicators, this committee supports the continual improvement of patient care at SJHMC. And the Risk Management Committee is in charge of developing and implementing all risk avoidance and management policies, procedures, processes, and improvements relating to risk surveillance, risk prevention, risk control, and unexpected events, identifying and evaluating important risk factors at least once a quarter helps providers prevent trends in patient harm outcomes while also improving their practice. They come to conclusions and take steps to improve the quality of their work in order to attain more success. Outside of the confines of an HCO, these medical management committees have other options for persuading health-care policymakers. They cooperate with other community HCOs at SJHMC in order to gain power in numbers and have their voices heard. With initiatives, they build an atmosphere that benefits the whole state. They're also renowned for reaching out to interested third parties in the business sector to assist fund their health-care reform efforts. In addition, administration members who are participating in these committees outside of their regular responsibilities lead and actively participate in multidisciplinary quality improvement initiatives as a significant contributor to SJHMC's public image and care. These committees are responsible for overseeing the quality and safety of patient treatment. SJHMC relies on these administrative executives to lead these committees in evaluating, reviewing, and improving procedures.

Managed care organizations roles and the future of health insurance:

Managed care organizations are the future of health insurance and play a significant role in health care administration and technology. They serve as a liaison between insurance companies and the government, expressing the patient's requirements to the managed care organization. I believe that managed care organizations would be extremely useful in that they would benefit not just me but also others. For example, managed care has aided me if I have to go to the hospital or have a doctor's appointment.

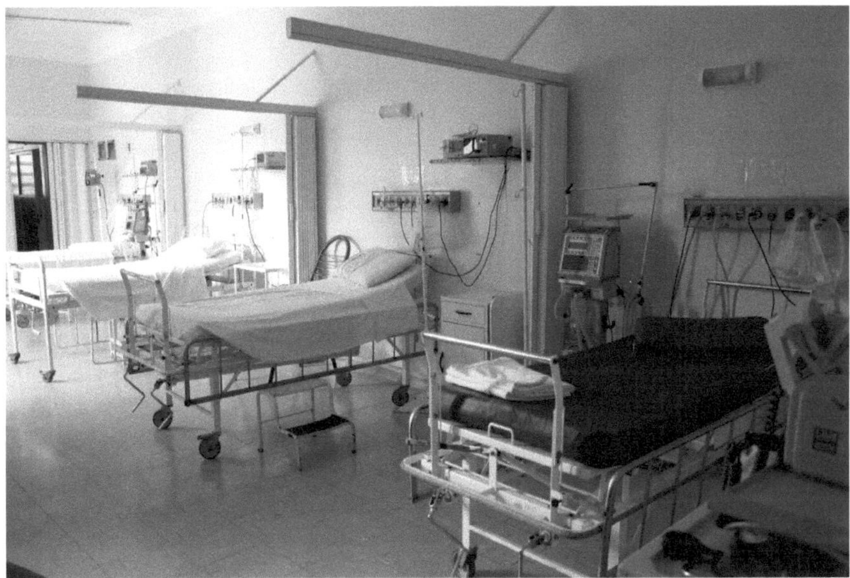

Figure No. 1 Healthcare System

They're the ones that talk to my doctors or physicians to figure out what kind of therapy I'll need and handle all of the financial arrangements that go along with it. Having a managed care plan, I believe, would save myself and others time and money. They participate in the legislative process at the national and state levels to push for new health insurance laws. They also litigate inside private sector advocacy campaigns for health care reform within the courts. As the number of people without health insurance in the United States rises, so does the need for health care. MCO's establishing public and political coalitions for change that would increase health insurance through tax credits has resulted in expanding health insurance and creating access to health care for every American. They also urge insurance companies to work toward a system that makes health insurance accessible to individuals and families. SJHMC is particularly concerned about the future of health-care insurance. Because CHW is a religiously sponsored nonprofit organization, they gave over $900 million in community benefits and free health care to the poor and low-income families in 2008.

The role of administration in health systems:

Information Technology is used by health care organizations to improve the quality, safety, efficacy, and efficiency of health care in various contexts, as well as to ensure continuity of treatment. The use of information technology in health care has been shown to improve health care in a number of big health-care delivery systems. IT investments must be in line with the goal and vision of the health-care institution. It is critical for the IT department to develop a Strategic Master Plan to assess the IT infrastructure and services available, including hardware, applications, manpower, and processes, in order to identify future needs and better understand any proposed technological investments by the various stakeholders in the organization.

The role of administration in health systems:

IT infrastructure in healthcare refers to the physical hardware that is used to run medical and business applications, such as networked medical instruments, enterprise storage systems, servers, desktops, laptops, and handheld devices, as well as interfaces, wired and wireless network devices, and connection media. The IT department at the hospital where I work underwent a significant upgrade in service delivery and IT infrastructure two years ago, creating compliance requirements with the Joint Commission International Accreditation and the College of American Pathologists. Starting major projects to enhance underlying infrastructure, such as the network, desktop computers, printers, laptops, servers, corporate data storage, and data centre reconfiguration to accommodate hospital growth while increasing the safety and security of IT resources.

The major two projects that were approved and implemented were:

ADT (admission, discharge, and transfer) and Physician Orders are made easier using the My Care-Cerner interface. ADT data is sent through the hospital network and kept in a central database. The interface allows the caregiver to input patient information into the computer, where ADT reads HL7 messages and changes the relevant database tables. Data is added, modified, cancelled, or removed in real time, and the ADT Interface Server gets a message and immediately updates the database for usage.

Some of the benefits of my-CARE-Cerner ADT Interface:

Saves time: patient information is stored in Cerner's patient master index and then automatically transferred to my CARE without having to re-enter the information. Reduced Data Entry Mistakes: With less data entered manually in my-CARE, there is a lower risk of data entry errors. Complete Patient Information: There is no need to explore other systems for information.

Figure No. 2 Healthcare Operations

Phase II of the ICIS-CERNER project required a significant code change to the underlying infrastructure in order to prepare for phase II. The following modules were included in Phase II Cerner: PharmNet is a data management system that organizes data, reduces duplication, and improves patient safety and communication among caregivers, physicians, and nurses by storing data just once, assuring efficiency and safety. SurginNet, which provides scheduling, thorough reporting, complete documentation for pre, intra, and post-operative procedures, case tracking, anesthetic documentation, and tools to automate the practice of anaesthesia to physicians, nurses, and surgical team members, and Profile, It allows for the integration of paper, document images, and electronic data into a single application, as well as chart completion, information release, and chart tracking. Other modules include CareNet, which connects a patient's electronic medical record to nursing activities, automatically documenting activities and streamlining communication between all members of the care team, and FirstNet, which was designed for emergency services and helps track the flow of patients from emergency departments to the ward or discharge, including the triaging stage.

Figure No. 3 Health Service & Operation System

Finally, the healthcare environment is not as straightforward as it appears. With all of the latest technology advancements and advances in medicine and research, many healthcare professionals must be ready to adapt to any new developments in the healthcare sector at all times. "One of the most important aspects of on-demand is that it enables a company to become not only more innovative, but also more efficient and responsive to change". As a result, the value of anybody working in the healthcare sector is defined by their ability to adapt to change, and if they can do so quickly, more patients will be happy with the service, and those physicians will be able to minimize problems that arise inside their workplace. This is why jobs in healthcare are vital in today's society, because the healthcare sector will undergo many changes in the future, and administrators must be prepared to adapt and gather as much knowledge as possible about new medications and cures when the time comes.

Chapter 2: About Hospitality Management

Hospitality & its History:

In terms of restaurant companies, the hospitality industry has become one of the largest employers in any country. It has risen to a greater status throughout the world and expects excellent work standards from its employees. There are several job options in this business, but they all demand the potential for personal skills in each subject. An employer looks for a variety of qualities, including a positive attitude, friendly demeanor, tidy appearance, desire to work, confidence, cleanliness, personal hygiene, efficiency, and honesty. Tourists play an important part in our hospitality business, since they are the primary market for restaurant services in the Philippines. They ensure that a visitor at a restaurant is attended to and that their requirements or desires are met. Filipinos are extremely kind and polite when it comes to ensuring that tourists/guests that dine and stay are entertained. Because there is so much rivalry in this sector right now, it has always been their responsibility to raise quality standards and improve service in order to give a better service.

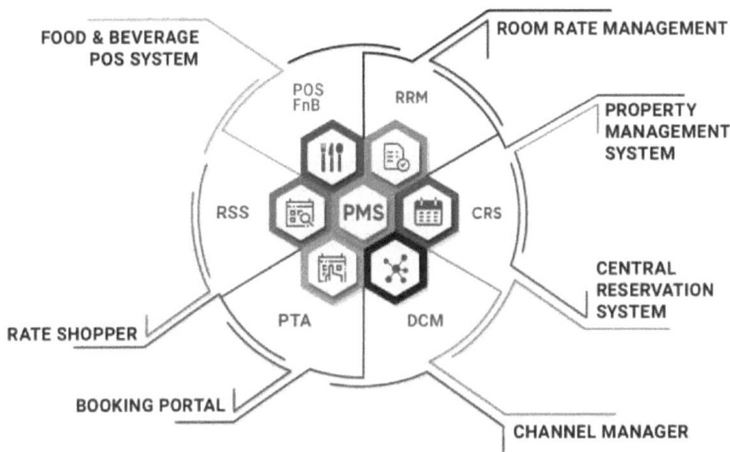

Figure No 4 Hospitality Systems
Source: https://www.cihms.com/en/a-new-approach-to-hospitality-management-solution-cihms-is-ready-for-the-world/

Restaurants are primarily concerned with food and drink. Customers will be served food and beverages by them. The sorts of tasks done by a food and beverage department vary greatly depending on the size of the restaurant, necessitating a wide range of abilities on the part of its employees. Conventions and catering are big business for most full-service restaurants. Small meeting rooms are used for meetings, whereas bigger rooms are used for general sessions, trade fairs, displays, or banquets. A restaurant's food service role can only be carried out efficiently if there is constant cooperation and coordination.

The marketing and sales departments, on the other hand, play a critical role in the restaurant industry, since its major goal is to sell and attract consumers based on the quality of their products. The work of the sales managers is divided according to the sort of client that a restaurant is seeking to attract.

Although the human resources department does not serve guests, it is critical to the smooth functioning of a restaurant. Employee recruiting, benefits, administration, and training are all handled by them. They are responsible for recruiting, interviewing, and screening potential workers.

In many restaurants, the accounting department mixes staff tasks with line functions, or those that deal with serving customers. Their job is to keep track of financial activities, create and evaluate financial statements, and deliver timely updates on operational outcomes to managers in other departments.

Efficiency, collaboration, and activity coordination within individual units are the most valuable elements of an organizational design. Every organization, including restaurants, is judged on its whole performance rather than the performance of a single department, and I believe that in order to reach every objective and become successful, strong leadership, initiative, collaboration, and coordination are required.

When questioned about the business climate in the Philippines, entrepreneurs agreed that, compared to other nations, it is relatively simpler to establish a firm here. It was allegedly less restricted in Manila. One of the factors that prevent many pinots from starting a company is a lack of self-esteem. Anyone with a little amount of money might simply try to make it on their own. Historically, the term "restaurant" exclusively applied to establishments that had tables at which customers could sit and eat their meals, and where the restaurant prepared and served food, drink, and dessert to customers who were generally served by a waiter. They come in a variety of shapes and sizes, with a vast range of cuisines and service methods. There are many different sorts of restaurants, from fast-food chains where food is ordered at a counter to sophisticated dine-in or sit-down restaurants that are typically classified as "family-style."

Restaurants take a variety of approaches to their products/services, including food, beverages, lodging, and a variety of other things. When opening a restaurant, the owner considers what to offer consumers, which is why the variety of products and services available varies depending on the type of restaurant.

One of our most fundamental requirements is food. Asian cuisine is one of the most unusual cuisines accessible. Many Westerners are growing increasingly interested in Asian cuisine in all of its colors and flavors. Cuisine in Asia stands out when compared to food on the American and European continents because of its diversity. A large number of Asian nations, many of which are geographically separated, provide a limitless variety of food. For example, Indian cuisine offers a diverse range of cuisines to sample, and even the most ardent foodie would need several lives to sample and appreciate them all. The Far East is another option. It is here that the greatest examples of Asian cuisine can be found, such as Japanese and Korean cuisine. While Asian cuisine is meant to be mainly rice-oriented, Chinese meals employ noodles instead of rice.

There are about 50,000 restaurant outlets in the domestic economy as of last year, with over 80% of them belonging to the fast food sub-sector. Food franchising is a very common business model. Over 1,500 franchised fast service restaurants, 24 casual dining and theme restaurants, and 600 coffee shops, bakeries, and confectioneries are located throughout the city. And the numbers continue to rise! In the Philippine food franchising business, American companies have a major presence. McDonald's, Shakey's, A&W; Burger King; Domino's; Kenny Roger's Roasters; KFC; Pizza Hut; Sbarro; Subways; Wendy's; California Pizza Kitchen; Hard Rock Cafe; Outback; TGIF; Italianism; Dairy Queen; Dunkin' Donuts; Wendy's; California Pizza Kitchen; Hard Rock Cafe; Outback; TGIF; Italianism; Dairy Queen; Dunkin'

The industry is characterized by low entry barriers. Franchisee capital investments might vary from PHP5, 000,000 to PHP10, 000,000. The franchisor arranges for training, marketing, and distribution networks. Franchisees do not need prior expertise or experience because the franchisor gives fully developed management and production systems to new entrants. These qualities of franchising, particularly in the food industry, make it highly appealing to new company owners.

The growth of one-stop shopping malls with a variety of recreational facilities and services, on the other hand, makes it easier for potential restaurant and fast food operators to enter the market. The restaurant sector saves money by not having to invest in comprehensive business development studies for its outlets because of these malls; mall magnates Henry Sy and John Gokongwei Jr. have a long track record of developing malls.

Consumer demand for every better product is rising in the restaurant and fast food business. The fast proliferation of food outlets in major regions of Metro Manila and the provinces demonstrates the boom. Fast food restaurants gained prominence in the 1980s, and the sector has continued to grow at double-digit rates in recent years.

In the restaurant industry, particularly in the fast food sub-sector, competition is strong. Although the market is huge, customers are price cautious and loyal to brands. With so many restaurants and fast food joints to select from, market share is determined by pricing systems and marketing techniques. As a result, industry participants' market strategies attempt to accomplish two major goals:

- Hammer in "value-for-money" notions, and
- Build brand awareness and loyalty.
- Pricing determines whether a restaurant's market share is gained or lost.
- Price reductions and discounts are frequently offered by industry companies to entice new consumers.

Furthermore, large players spend a lot of money on advertising to build brand awareness and loyalty. Raffle drawings, free gift items, and highly treasured meal combos, as well as reduced toys and school supplies for every set minimum food purchase, are all examples of marketing techniques. The goal of celebrity endorsements is for the market to identify with the endorser.

Similarly, fierce rivalry forces businesses to develop new items in order to gain a larger part of the market. Restaurateurs' must be on the lookout for the newest culinary and wine creations, both domestically and internationally, and adapt those to local tastes. Several fast-food restaurants that normally provide solely western food have included dishes that appeal to the Filipino appetite.

Raising quality standards and enhancing service, particularly in the fast food sub-sector, have also been key focuses of competitiveness. Players provide incentives and compensations to workers in order to encourage them to be more productive at work and therefore contribute to the fast food outlet's high standards of excellent service and cleanliness. In a fast food or restaurant, pleasant and friendly employees are also essential. Not surprisingly, one of the most important characteristics that consumers demand from a fast food business is quick service.

Restaurant and fast food operators must combine marketing considerations with growing operating expenses, particularly those associated with imported food components. Profit margin erosion is generally addressed by raising final product/service prices or cutting shortcuts in manufacturing or service delivery. Either option might lead to a decrease in client base.

Size and Scope of the Sector:

The 14 sectors included by the category range from hotels and restaurants to events, gaming, and travel services. In the United Kingdom, there are roughly 146,000 unique hospitality, leisure, travel, and tourist businesses, with pubs, bars, and nightclubs accounting for 43% and restaurants accounting for 34%. Small and medium-sized businesses dominate the industry 71%. They do, however, make up just 53% of the workforce. Firms with more than 250 employees make up less than 1% of all businesses, yet they employ 43% of the workforce.

Productivity:

The industry has the lowest labor productivity of any in the UK economy, with a comparable service sector (retail) having doubled the sector's labor productivity. It is lagging behind its foreign rivals. In comparison to the UK industry, labor productivity in the United States is about a third greater and nearly twice in France.

Workforce:

Nearly two million individuals work in the industry. Restaurants employ almost half a million people (32 percent of the workforce), followed by pubs, bars, and nightclubs (18 percent), and hotels (14 percent) (14 percent). The industry is well-represented throughout the United Kingdom. However, England employs the most people in the industry (83 percent).
With 15% of employees aged 16-19 and another 31% aged 20-29, the industry employs a young workforce. Ethnic minorities make about 14% of the workforce, which is more than the national

average. Full-time employees account for 55% of the workforce. One-fifth of the sector's workforce (or 20%) is foreign-born. In London, this figure climbs to 62 percent.

Core Occupation:

The sector employs a significant number of core (industry-specific) and non-core (non-industry-specific) jobs (found in most sectors). The following table shows the number of people employed in the sector's

Key occupations:

- Assistants in the kitchen and catering (394,600)
- Chefs and chefs de cuisine (255,100)
- Bartenders (197,800)
- Managers of restaurants and caterers (148,200)
- Managers of hotels and lodging (57,700)
- Managers and publicans of licenced establishments (46,900)
- Consultants in travel (47,500)
- Attendants at leisure and theme parks (17,900)
- Tour guides and travel agents (15,900)
- Managers of conferences and exhibitions (23,700)
- Porters at hotels (11,300)
- Managers of travel agencies (9,000)

Hard to fill vacancies and skill shortages:

Vacancies are reported by 17 percent of sector businesses, with 32 percent of them being difficult to fill. 66 percent of these openings are difficult to fill due to a shortage of qualified candidates. Employers indicate that candidates lack customer service skills 50 percent of the time, teamwork skills 47 percent of the time, oral communication skills 43 percent of the time, and problem solving abilities 39 percent of the time.

Labor Turnover:

The overall turnover rate in the industry is about 31%. (Although large employers sometimes report double or even treble this figure). This costs the sector £414 million each year, based on an average recruiting and first training cost of £673. Only 17% of businesses, on the other hand, believe their labor turnover is excessive.

Skills Gaps:

The workforce is made up of 11% of people who have no credentials. Only 12% of hotel and lodging managers, 7% of restaurant managers, and 6% of publicans and licensed establishments managers have any qualifications. Chefs with no credentials make about 10% of the skilled trade's workforce. In comparison to 19% of all firms, 26% of businesses in the sector report having personnel that are not completely skilled to fulfill the demands of their business.

Training and Development:

Employers who provide training increased from 61 percent in 2005 to 66 percent in 2007 and 68 percent in 2009. In terms of training techniques, most businesses provide informal training to their employees, with introductory/induction training also being widely available. Training is far more likely to be provided by large operators. Supervisors are the most likely to receive training, followed by bar and waiting personnel. Cleaning employees, housekeepers, and room attendants are the least likely to receive training.

Industries Covered:

Events, food and beverage management, gambling, amusement parks, hospitality services, hostels, and hotels are just a few examples.

Membership Clubs:

Restaurants, pubs, bars, and nightclubs Tourist services, travel services, and visitor attractions are all examples of self-catering accommodations.

British Hospitality Association:

The BHA is the hospitality industry's largest trade association, representing hotels, restaurants, and food service companies. Aim to provide tangible benefits to members by proactively supporting the industry's interests via collaborations with government and other groups and organizations. This organization has selected five major areas in which they will play a leading role in industry action and change, including First, the economy—to advocate for a budgetary climate that will allow the sector to thrive in the face of global competition, second, employment—bridging the gap between education and industry and developing a competent hospitality workforce, third, intelligent regulation, which advises governments on how to decrease the expense of costly regulation at both the national and local levels. The fourth is Sustainability, which involves enabling an industry-led effort to achieve short- and long-term economic, social, and environmental success, finally, Health-proactively promoting industry and public sector policies to improve our customers' well-being. In summary, the BHA's goal is to

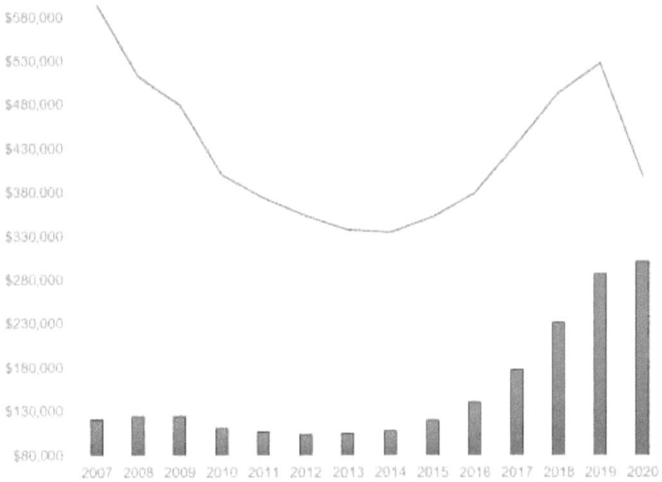

Figure No. 5 British Hospitality Associations Metrics
Source: https://www.altusgroup.com/services/insights/executive-summary-british-columbia-hotel-association-webinar/

Provide concrete, long-term, positive advantages to each member's business through collective efforts.

Restaurant Staffing and Structures:

The restaurant industry is structured in a hierarchical manner. Everyone has a title and a job to do, much like in the army. Managers and Executive Chefs are at the top, while busboys and dishwashers are at the bottom. The restaurant's workforce structure will be determined by the idea. There will be no Executive Chef or Sommelier in a coffee shop (wine manager) .They should be a staff for both the kitchen and the dining area to manage a good restaurant. If the business is huge, more people will be needed in both sectors. A head chef is needed in the kitchen to coordinate and supervise food preparation. When the head chef is off duty, a sous chef is assigned to look after the kitchen. Cooking and plating will be done by line cooks. Prep cooks must ensure that the kitchen is properly prepared for any circumstance that may arise. To do the dishes and work on peeling veggies, you'll need a dishwasher. Bus passengers are required to remove and set tables in the eating area. Customers' orders are taken to the kitchen by waitresses, who then deliver the cooked meal, a front-end manager to assist with any issues and oversee the waitresses and bus employees on the spot.

Customers' health and safety are the responsibility of all employees. Host/Hostess is in charge of welcoming clients at the entrance, keeping track of how many people are seated where and balancing the workload of the wait staff, managing bookings and those in line, and escorting them to their seats 7 while ensuring that they have menus. He or she is in charge of the wait crew.

Wait staff is in charge of ensuring that the table is clean and set with clean utensils in the proper configuration, greeting customers at their tables in a timely manner, ensuring that customers have drinks and enough time to decide on their order, accurately taking that order, and conveying it to the kitchen. Responsible for keeping an eye on their tables and making sure their customers have drinks and are generally happy; responsible for getting food from the kitchen when it's ready and getting it to the customers without spilling it or touching them unless it's absolutely necessary; responsible for getting food from the kitchen when it's ready and getting it to the customers without spilling it or touching them unless it's absolutely necessary; responsible for getting food from the kitchen when it's ready and getting it to the customers without spilling it or Responsible for ensuring that all meals are to the customer's satisfaction before moving out of the way while they eat. When customers have finished dining, return to clear the table and inquire if they require any more services; wash, rinse, and repeat until the client requests a bill. Before giving the ill to the client, wait staff must ensure that it is accurate.

Cook: Inspects the kitchen before starting to cook to ensure it meets food safety guidelines, inspects all food items before using for any signs of cross contamination or spoilage, prepares food according to food safety preparation guidelines, including cooking temperatures and times, and arranges food on the plate in a pleasing manner. Dishwashers are under his supervision. Dishwashers are in charge of ensuring that all silverware, flatware, and cooking equipment is cleaned properly with the correct quantity of cleanser at the right temperature for the right amount of time in order to preserve hygiene and avoid disease transmission.

Cleaning crew: responsible for overall restaurant sanitation - far more crucial than most people realize, a good janitorial team can keep a restaurant up to health code and avert severe litigation by upholding the business's cleanliness standards. Most restaurants do not have a distinct job for this, and instead combine these responsibilities with those of the wait crew without giving further training. Manager: ensures that all employees are performing their duties, counsels employees on areas where they excel and where they need to improve, hires and fires as needed, monitors customer satisfaction, and handles all paperwork, including ensuring that the building meets all safety codes and standards. Responsible for employee morale and overall restaurant productivity; may also be in charge of ad placement.

Over the next few years, the most pressing operational problem in the foodservice industry will be how to manage and develop a multicultural and intergenerational workforce. According to J. Sullivan, who was addressing industry concerns, 40% of all restaurant staff are under the age of 25, and 28% do not speak English at home. All of this is contingent on the hiring, recruitment, performance, and training of employees.

The food service and restaurant sector nowadays is a highly specialized industry with its own set of legislative requirements. To stay afloat in today's economic climate, wise restaurant and company owners seek legal advice before problems occur. Manage food and beverage licensing and distribution agreements, franchise agreements, and supplier contracts, as well as assist restaurant owners with the purchase and sale of existing restaurants, lease negotiations, and risk management. Finally, assist with a variety of employment issues ranging from management training to employment disputes.

Restaurant Standard Operation Procedures (SOP) are frequently utilized to assist most restaurant owners and managers in managing and guiding the whole restaurant team and employees in order to improve service performance and achieve the business's overall objectives and goals. It is difficult to provide the best service standards of what the client wants and expects to the restaurant if the business has a comprehensive training manual or SOP for the employees. A reputable and well-managed restaurant should give a weekly or bi-weekly training programmed for all employees, covering each restaurant operation method. I am confident that performing many training sessions will make it much easier for a restaurant to maintain the efficacy and efficiency of its service operation. To make things simple and easy to grasp once again,

As a result of new restaurant franchising regulations, many individuals believe that seeing nutritional information printed next to menu items will encourage them to make healthier choices. Others, on the other hand, concede that it will have no impact on their menu selections. Consumers, on the other hand, appear to be generally in favor of the new legislation.

The government of the United Kingdom has stated that calorie counts for food sold in takeaways, restaurant franchises, and canteens would be tested. It is looking for volunteer firms to show calorie content information and believes that if a standardized guide is agreed upon, the rest of the industry will rapidly follow suit. To summaries, there are few women managers in the hospitality sector in the United Kingdom, particularly in the restaurant industry, due to a variety of causes - historical, traditional, sociological, and even personal in character. Regardless of other circumstances, the theoretical frameworks that underpin the topic are reliant on every woman employee's duty. Employers must recognize their efforts in achieving the position they deserve. They do, in fact, have a major role in the corporate hierarchy. Men and women workers will be on an equal footing as a result of this.

It's fairly unusual to totally transform the look of an established restaurant. This may be due to new owners, or it could just be because the present owner wants to shake things up. It could be time for a change if the restaurant hasn't been performing well. Begin with a strategy. Take your time to iron out all the details, from paint colors to seating arrangements, and everything will go well. You may just work from the list once you've made a plan.

Before implementing a change, conduct market research by conducting a survey or other kind of study to see what people enjoy and whether or not they will desire the change. Research can be expensive, but it is still less expensive than altering everything only to discover there is no market for it. Any business and restaurants in particular, require a great deal of research. Also, inform your clients.

If people are unaware that their image is changing, they may feel uneasy and uncomfortable. As a result, make sure it's part of your marketing plan. Promote the fact that the restaurant is going to be remodeled and enhanced, as well as why it will be better and what guests may expect. This is especially true if not just the image but also the menu will undergo significant modifications. Furthermore, altering the restaurant's whole image can have a significant impact on business, so think it through carefully beforehand. To ensure that what has been done is a superior concept, market research is conducted.

Food is very much a component of popular culture, and a society's eating habits are influenced by its beliefs, customs, and trends. The ideas and things created by a society, including commercial, political, media, and other systems, as well as the influence of these ideas and products on society, are referred to as popular culture.

Current Eating Trends:

More individuals dining out; the use of dietary and herbal supplements; foods for certain groups (e.g., dieters, women, sports, older persons); the use of convenience and functional foods; and ethnic variety in diets are all examples of consumerism. In industrialized nations, the general public prefers low-calorie, low-fat cuisine made with simple, natural, and fresh ingredients. Diets have been "Americanized" throughout the world as fast-food outlets and convenience foods have grown in popularity. Some essential foods are still needed in underdeveloped nations, and governments and the food industry are striving to produce solutions that can help alleviate worldwide food shortages and nutritional deficiency issues.

Eating Away from Home:

Since the second part of the twentieth century, the share of money spent on meals consumed away from home, as well as the number of restaurants, has been continuously growing. People can eat in formal sit-down restaurants, fast-food restaurants, cafés, or buy food from street sellers. Fast-food restaurants have grown quite popular, and people of all ages frequent them. The "McDonaldization" of America refers to the rapid expansion and popularity of fast food. Consumption of these eateries has declined significantly among heavy users aged 18 to 34, but has grown among other groups. Their appeal has grown on a global scale as well.

This simple dinner exemplifies the complex link that exists between a culture and its cuisine. The fast-food burger was popularized in the twentieth century as a result of a demand for quick, portable meals. The prevalence of fast food has contributed to an obesity pandemic throughout time, for a small additional cost (a "super size"), many restaurants now offer bigger dish (portion) sizes. Obesity has been related to eating out from home and a change to a more sedentary lifestyle.

Dieting:

People buy weight reduction pills, herbal supplements, and specially created weight loss drinks, meals, and diet bars in order to lose weight. In order to reduce weight and improve their health, people also join health clubs or spas or purchase specialized weight loss and exercise equipment. Food-focused, celebrity, exchange, and supplement-based diets are some of the most popular types of diets. Food-focused diets stress the intake of only one or a few foods, such as the grapefruit diet, banana diet, or wine drinker's diet. Exchange plans group together items with similar calories, carbohydrates, proteins, and fats into food groups. Celebrity plans generally have the backing of a celebrity, and celebrity plans lump together items with similar calories, carbohydrates, proteins, and fats into food groups. Some diets require the purchase of a commercial meal, snack bar, food, or beverage.

Supplements:

Nutrient- and other-ingredient pills, liquids, and powders are now widely available in supermarkets. Herbal supplements (or herbal components) are becoming increasingly popular. Supplement production and use, on the other hand, are not usually highly regulated, so consumers must be cautious about what they buy and eat.

Convenience Foods:

Many restaurants offer take-out meals or things to please people who want to dine properly at home but don't have time or don't want to make complicated dinners. Convenience foods are defined as fully or partially prepared "TOTE" (take-out-to-eat) foods, which include home-delivered meals. People's desire to save time, as well as their use of convenience foods, grows when more women (traditional family dinner preparers) enter the workforce.

Ethnic Foods:

People now consume dishes from civilizations other than their own. However, during the late twentieth century, ethnic cuisines, such as those from Asia, the Middle East, and Latin America, have become more widely consumed. This development is part of a larger trend toward greater diversity in all facets of life.

Functional Foods:

The phrase "functional food" refers to foods that contain nutrients (or non-nutrients) that may help to prevent disease. Foods that have been fortified have certain photochemical or active microbes added, or have been made through genetic engineering techniques are referred to as fortified foods. All foods, however, can help with health in some way, and there is no legal definition of functional food. Furthermore, the real benefit of these foods, if any, is subject to interpretation.

Chapter 3: Health care management and its importance

Healthcare management encompasses a wide range of occupations, and these leadership and management responsibilities are required in all fields of healthcare. The following are some examples of healthcare management positions:

- Coordinators of health

This position is most commonly found in hospitals and nursing homes, and it is in charge of assessing and monitoring the quality of care delivered in their service area. A health coordinator's responsibilities include developing patient care plans, documenting the treatment done, and ordering any necessary medical supplies.

- Clinical supervisors

A clinical director's function is applicable to many aspects of healthcare, including hospitals, nursing homes, research institutes, and clinics. Clinical directors are in charge of managing and guiding their teams of employees in order to achieve the organization's overall objectives.
Their responsibilities include formulating departmental goals, creating staff procedures, and employing additional employees as needed.

- Managers of hospitals

Hospital management positions can be found in a variety of settings, including hospitals, clinics, and private practices. Hospital executives are in charge of the entire hospital; therefore they have a wide range of tasks.

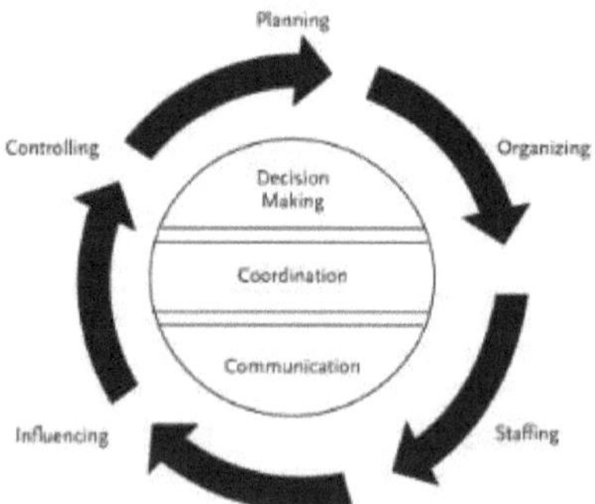

Figure No. 6 Important of Healthcare Management

You may anticipate spending your days as a hospital manager supervising finances, engaging with stakeholders and investors, and ensuring compliance with laws and regulations.

Supervisors of health

Health supervisory positions are available at care facilities and health service providers, and the position is similar to that of a healthcare administrator, which we'll discuss later. They usually work in emergency rooms and hospitals, where they are in charge of a variety of administrative chores. A health supervisor, for example, can anticipate maintaining track of data in databases, record information, attending meetings and reporting back, making staff schedules, and design staff schedules.

It's crucial to keep in mind that the responsibilities and tasks of each of these roles might vary significantly based on the size and type of organization in which you work. All of them, however, are incredibly significant and fulfilling careers.

What does healthcare management involve?

Now that we've defined the phrase, let's look at what healthcare management entails. Because the healthcare business is always changing and improving, it's critical to stay on top of things and ensure that every aspect of a hospital or similar institution is in good working order. Non-clinical activities inside the relevant healthcare establishment are planned, directed, and coordinated. Budgeting and financial management for the entire healthcare system. The establishment of work schedules for all employees, as well as the scheduling of new employees. Individual departments are overseen to ensure that they function smoothly and efficiently. Maintaining patient happiness and well-being through doing quality assurance and risk assessment tasks. All employees, including caretakers, physicians, and providers, are under strict monitoring.

What does a healthcare manager do?

May be incredibly profitable, and there are several possibilities to consider. Those who wish to make a difference and work in the healthcare business but in a less clinical setting might consider becoming a healthcare manager. Let's look at some of a healthcare manager's general responsibilities. Budgets should be optimized, and general financial issues should be addressed. Define the goals and build plans and tactics to achieve them. Attend numerous meetings and report back to the employees Oversee the hospital or department's day-to-day activities keep in touch with your stakeholder's .Handle any concerns that emerge, and deal with change in the healthcare institution properly.

Why is healthcare management important?

Healthcare management is a critical component of a properly working hospital or healthcare organization, and the sector would not be able to run efficiently without it. But what is it about management that makes it so important? It's no secret that under the right management, a business or organization may prosper, but leadership and management in healthcare is especially vital. While other sectors supply products and services, healthcare stands apart because it delivers things and services that save lives. The healthcare industry's services and products help people avoid suffering, treat illnesses, and maybe save their lives. As a result, effective leadership strategies are essential for ensuring that everything is done correctly and that everyone is safe. Experts in the area of healthcare are required to remain on top of changes in laws and regulations, as well as medical developments, in order to provide the best possible treatment. Because the sector is always evolving and progressing, management is required to steer medical centers and hospitals in the appropriate path.

Healthcare industry growth:

Determining when to recruit new professionals inside clinics and hospitals, for example, is crucial to healthcare administration.

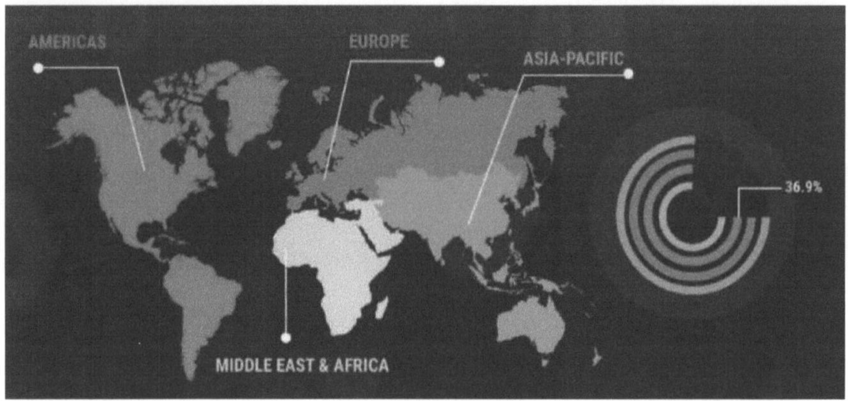

Figure No. 7 Industry Growth
Source: www.medgadget.com/2019/12/home-healthcare-market-size-share-2019

As the world's population grows, so does the number of people working in the business. Between 2020 and 2021, the number of personnel in the NHS increased by 2.9 percent, or 37,488 people. Despite the fact that staff numbers normally expand each year, COVID-19 has resulted in a massive increase in workload and personnel numbers in the healthcare business in recent years. Hospitals were already overburdened with sick patients, and the requirement for a vaccine, as well as its administration, added to the effort and strain on employees. Healthcare professionals encounter several obstacles on a daily basis, and having the right management in place may help to alleviate these difficulties. It's only natural that healthcare occupations would continue to develop as the sector grows. Between 2019 and 2029, employment is expected to expand by 32%, which is much quicker than most other professional options. It's evident that healthcare management's role in the sector is critical, and it entails a slew of significant jobs and obstacles. We hope that this article has helped you gain a better grasp of this important aspect of healthcare.

Chapter 4: Hospitality Management and its Importance.

Individual departments are overseen to ensure that they run smoothly and efficiently. Maintaining patient happiness and well-being through performing quality assurance and risk assessment tasks. All employees, including caretakers, doctors, and providers, are under strict monitoring. Check out our amazing healthcare management and leadership principles course if you're interested in learning more about healthcare management. A healthcare manager must be employed at every business within the industry in order to carry out these critical functions. If you're considering a career as a healthcare manager, we've put together a handy 'how to become a healthcare manager' guide that includes a wealth of information. In a moment, we'll go over some of the major ideas from the guide.

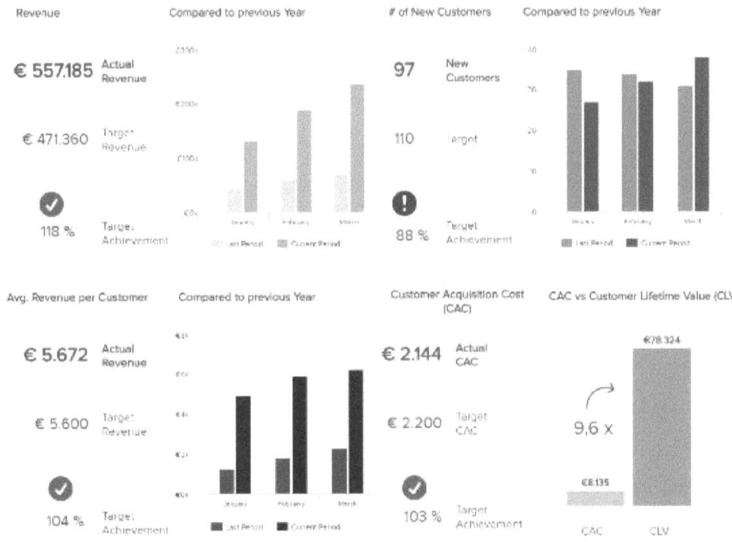

Figure No. 8 Importance of Hospitality
Source: https://www.datapine.com/blog/how-to-create-sql-dashboards/

The healthcare profession is very tempting, but as we've already established, management is a very different experience than working directly with patients as a nurse or surgeon. It's an intriguing combination of working in a company and a medical setting. Management is becoming increasingly important in today's ever-changing world. Effective managers must "promote work improvement, enhance learning, and challenge people" to handle challenges in novel ways1. This is especially true in the realm of hospitality. As a general manager of a hotel, you must have a suitable leadership style, the capacity to control your ego, and the desire to innovate in the field1. In today's constantly changing lodging business, hospitality manager's face a variety of issues.

In particular, all hotel general managers will have to deal with emotional confrontations, make unpleasant decisions, and understand the tradeoffs that must be made in day-to-day operations.
In addition, hospitality managers must be able to adjust to changing market trends. One noteworthy trend is that millennial "have very different expectations of the hospitality industry than previous generations;" more specifically, they are not typically loyal to one specific brand of accommodations, preferring instead to seek out "unique rather than familiar" products, services, and experiences, referring to brands owned by major players such as Hilton, Marriott, and Choice Hotels.

Furthermore, today's hospitality executives must incorporate technology with the goal of giving a modern lodging experience. A robotic arm known as the "Yobot" handles guest luggage in place of human bellhops at the flagship of the relatively new Yotel chain in New York City2. This forward-thinking hotel also features motorized, rolling beds, which save space in each of its rooms. Hotel management must execute plans that integrate technological improvements into the hotel's business, but more significantly, into the guest experience, with the hopes of improving guests' opinions and earning repeat business as a result of the increase of technology in accommodations.

 Data mining procedures have spread across numerous businesses on a global basis, and they have proven to be advantageous in the hotel industry. Hoteliers can now "tailor their marketing materials to particular consumer preferences," boosting their customers' experiences2. As a result, it is critical for accommodation managers to design tactics for connecting with their customers while also giving new and unique experiences with each stay. Ramapo College of New Jersey's Center for Innovative and Professional Learning offers a certificate degree in hospitality and restaurant management for working individuals interested in pursuing a career in the management of hotels, motels, and inns across the country and across the world (CIPL). Students in the programmed will learn the fundamental principles of lodging and restaurant management that are required for success in the industry, as well as how to implement these concepts in hotels and restaurants. Ramapo's CIPL programmer is designed to prepare professionals to pursue lucrative opportunities in an evolving field, with workshops ranging from effective team management, professional communication, and service excellence to service operations management and finance for lodging and restaurant managers

Chapter 5: Innovative Implementation in the Health Care Management.

A healthcare organization's capacity to incorporate innovative procedures is heavily reliant on its people, particularly its management. Middle managers are valued highly because they provide as a link between upper management and nursing staff. Researchers studied the behavior of a number of hospital executives and identified patterns of behavior that are likely to aid healthcare companies in more effectively implementing new procedures.

Figure No. 9 Technology in Healthcare
Source: https://www.globalgrowth.com/healthcare-technology-group/

The most important aspect of updating healthcare organizations working procedures is teaching workers to use new machinery and techniques and assisting them in dealing with new challenges. Researchers, according to them, have undervalued and overlooked the importance of middle managers in this process, which is why they decided to look into it. They developed a classification of managers' contributions to the implementation of innovations by studying qualitative data from healthcare companies and interviewing individuals.

Manager's Responsibilities:

The authors present a list of recommended techniques for managers at the end of the paper, including informal communication, persuading employees to accept innovations, and integrating training to real projects. As a result, the article's worth is that it discusses the relevance of managers in enhancing organizational processes and offers ways for implementing new practices efficiently. Managers should "help staff members by ensuring they have the information and resources needed to conduct improvement implementation and resolve any impediments staff experience," according to a strategy. Because I work as a radiologic technologist at a large hospital, this practice is really important to me. Employees in the department operate a variety of radiographic equipment that, in the event of misconduct or equipment failure, could damage patients or medical workers. As a result, personnel must ensure that they are competent to operate with mechanisms such as an MRI scanner or an X-ray machine, as well as the ability to notice when they are malfunctioning. This technique requires managers to assure not only the availability of appropriate equipment, but also the training of employees and the resolution of any difficulties that arise.

Implementing Innovative Practices:

My manager utilizes this practice in a variety of ways. First and foremost, he oversees radiologic technologists' work on a daily basis and ensures that they have access to the equipment they need to do their jobs. Following that, he ensures that the personnel receives adequate assistance in learning to operate the equipment and dealing with any problems that may arise. My boss is also concerned about employee safety, ensuring that they are exposed to the least amount of radiation possible while operating the equipment. He pays close attention to his colleagues' concerns and assists them in dealing with work-related issues. These acts create a positive organizational climate in which employees are encouraged to uphold corporate principles and participate in the implementation of new ideas. My boss is also concerned about my staff' ability to receive training and improve their qualifications. Acquiring, maintaining, and developing competence is critical in healthcare professionals' work because it helps them to operate technology, identify potential causes of error, and notice inconsistencies in the results. As a result, my boss is concerned about his employees' professional achievement. He encourages them to continue their studies and earn as many diplomas as they can. Workers receive up to $5000 each year to support their college fees for this purpose. Furthermore, when employees are overworked and fail to complete their board exams on time, the manager consults with doctors. As a result, he guarantees that personnel have the necessary qualifications to do their jobs.

Finally the head deals with issues that arise during personnel's working hours and in their interactions with patients. He tries to diffuse the situation when personnel fall behind on their duties, making inpatients or outpatients wait for long periods of time and become unhappy or worried. He could, for example, provide them with a free meal in the cafeteria or free parking. My boss aims to give workers the highest pay boost possible, in addition to lowering friction between staff and patients. My manager has implemented one of the tactics given in the article, thus it is feasible to assess its effectiveness in terms of implementing innovations. According to Libeler and McConnell, a manager's job is to increase staff efficiency and focus their efforts toward the organization's goals. In this way, the stated practice's application is in line with managerial goals. Providing employees with the required equipment, pushing them to get as much training as possible, and educating them how to cope with challenges in the workplace not only boosts productivity but also promotes employee loyalty. These activities establish an environment that encourages employees to accept organizational changes and participate in the implementation of new ideas.

Chapter 6: Innovative Implementations in Hospitality Management.

According to research, the hospitality business is becoming more competitive. This means that in order to be competitive, various industry companies must keep present clients while also attracting new ones. This entails providing high-quality services that match the increasingly sophisticated needs of customers. Tourists are looking for new and different experiences.

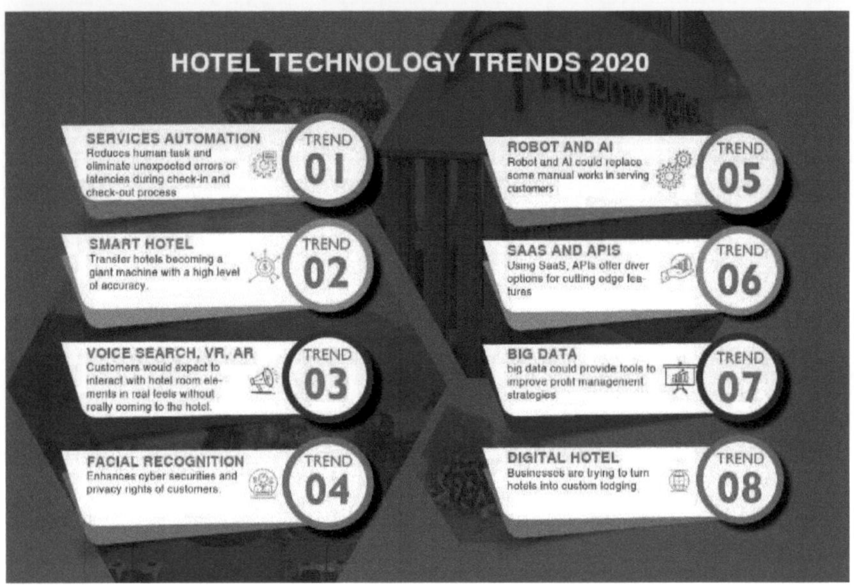

Figure No. 10 Technology in Hospitality

Organizational Teams:

Organizations are increasingly emphasizing teamwork as a means of addressing these new issues. As a result, a growing number of businesses in the hotel industry are forming organizational teams. This pattern leads me to believe that information sharing and team culture has a significant impact on service innovation in the hotel business. Organizational teams are increasingly exchanging their ideas and experiences with one another. As a result, new and innovative products that improve consumer happiness have been developed. As a result, there is widespread agreement that information is a critical component of every business's success. Knowledge management and knowledge sharing are crucial aspects of organizational success, according to recent research studies.

Knowledge Management and Sharing:

Knowledge management is a social process that takes into account a number of social and cultural elements. Any company's capacity to establish a competitive edge is determined by its ability to incorporate staff knowledge, skills, and expertise into daily management procedures. This entails the sharing of knowledge as well as the application of that knowledge. The most crucial aspect in the adoption of a knowledge management system within an organization, according to sharing. Organizations, on the other hand, can improve knowledge sharing by using technology, engaging people, and cultivating a collaborative culture (Yang, 2007). Leadership and organizational communication can also help an organization improve knowledge sharing. Because they improve service innovation, these methods are helpful for firms in the hospitality industry.

Hotels can increase service quality through boosting employee knowledge of customer preferences and improving service quality. Despite the tremendous benefits of knowledge sharing, there are a number of obstacles to overcome. Employees may hoard knowledge, which is a common problem. Chefs, for example, may find themselves in a lot of rivalry and begin to develop secret recipes. During team meetings, they may forget to discuss these recipes. Another issue is partial knowledge transfer, in which employees give only a portion of their knowledge rather than all of it. It is extremely difficult for most firms to eliminate information hoarding. Chefs, for example, may find themselves in a lot of rivalry and begin to develop secret recipes. During team meetings, they may forget to discuss these recipes. Another issue is partial knowledge transfer, in which employees give only a portion of their knowledge rather than all of it. It is extremely difficult for most firms to eliminate information hoarding. As a result, businesses must discover how to motivate individuals to share their knowledge. Organizations can improve member sharing by cultivating a pleasant team culture that encourages healthy collaboration.

Team Culture:

Most firms in the hospitality industry rely on teamwork to succeed. The simple rules, conventions, roles, and expectations that members of a team share and endorse are referred to as team culture. A culture is a mental construct that provides an organization's members with a shared feeling of identity. Using the overlapping traits of team members, hospitality firms can create a strong team culture. Organizations can also generate a team culture by examining team member interaction patterns. As a result, team culture allows members of a group to assess themselves as well as form team relationships. Strategic intent is a key component that can help teams collaborate more effectively when it comes to innovation. It also improves communication and social interaction, as well as motivating employees. The interactions between diverse members of the organization create a team culture. The strength of a team culture, on the other hand, is determined by how many individuals of an organization share the same rules, expectations, and duties Members should have overlapping traits, even if it is not required that they share these rules and standards. Because joint member expectations enable inventive performance, an innovative team has a strong culture. In this scenario, the quality of a concept is critical to the success of new services.

Managerial Implications:

The importance of employees is revealed in studies on the influence of information sharing and team culture on service innovation performance in the hotel industry. Employees are the most valuable assets of a company, according to this analysis. It is obvious that knowledge sharing is the most effective strategy for hospitality firms to attain high levels of service innovation. Furthermore, a positive team culture denotes a high level of service innovation in a firm. This is due to the fact that a team culture with organizational support, coherence, and cooperation can promote knowledge sharing. Individual members of organizations are likewise motivated and empowered by such a culture. As a result, the firm will be successful in motivating all team members to provide high-quality services.

This implies that managers should show concern for both the needs of employees and customers. The findings of this research can assist managers to understand the importance of soft elements of knowledge sharing and team culture. However, the mixed results of knowledge sharing imply that managers need to understand the relationship between various configurations of team culture and knowledge sharing. The strong effects of team culture and knowledge sharing suggest that managers should improve organization culture and enhance interactions. The fact that service innovation leads to customer satisfaction also suggests that managers need to create strong innovative cultures

This means that managers should be concerned about both staff and customer demands. The outcomes of this study can help managers appreciate the value of soft factors like knowledge sharing and team culture. However, given the mixed effects of information sharing, managers must comprehend the relationship between distinct team culture configurations and knowledge sharing. Because of the substantial effects of team culture and information sharing, managers should work to improve the culture of their organizations and improve relationships. The fact that service innovation leads to increased customer satisfaction implies that managers must foster strong inventive cultures.

Chapter 7: Artificial intelligence in health care and hospitality

Intelligence in hospitality:

Artificial intelligence, or AI, is the ability of computers or machines to undertake seemingly intelligent actions. Artificial intelligence has been around since the 1950s, but technology has only recently improved to the point where it can be regarded dependable enough to use for critical commercial activities. AI, in its most basic form, refers to computers or machines that do tasks that were previously assumed to require cognitive function. It is linked to ideas such as automation and big data, artificial Intelligence Becoming Important in the Hospitality Industry.

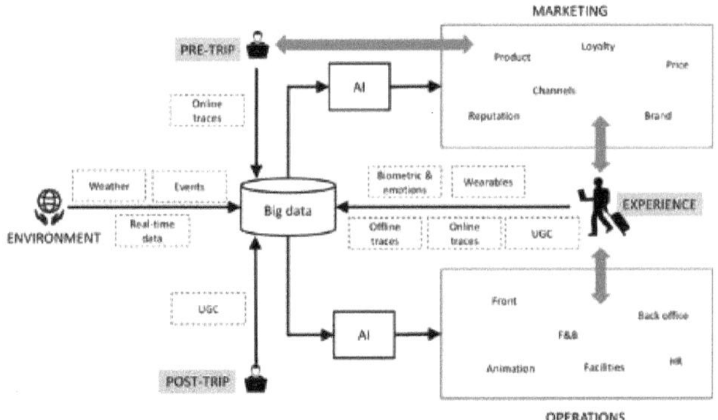

Figure No. 11 Data Generation & AI Technology

Artificial intelligence may now be used for a wide range of jobs, from basic customer service to personalization duties, more advanced problem-solving and even sales procedures and direct messaging, thanks to advances in computer technology and the collecting of client data. Examples of How to Use Artificial Intelligence within the Hospitality Industry Artificial intelligence is playing an increasingly important role in hospitality management, primarily because of its ability to carry out traditionally human functions at any time of the day. This potentially means that hotel owners can save significant money, eliminate human error and deliver superior service.

In particular, customer service is a vital part of the travel industry, with hotels often living and dying based on the way they treat their customers. With artificial intelligence, the possibilities for improving this aspect are almost endless, ranging from increased personalization to tailored recommendations. Artificial intelligence is becoming increasingly significant in the hotel industry, owing to its capacity to do traditionally human tasks at any time of day. This might save hoteliers a lot of money, minimize human mistake, and allow them to provide better service.

Customer service is especially important in the travel sector, as hotels often live or die dependent on how they serve their clients. The options for increasing this element with artificial intelligence are nearly unlimited, ranging from improved personalization to personalized recommendations. Despite the fact that artificial intelligence is still in its infancy in the hotel sector, it already has a number of practical uses, some of which are detailed below.

In-Person Customer Service:

The use of artificial intelligence to give in-person customer service is an example of artificial intelligence in the hotel business. Robots with artificial intelligence are already being developed, and the potential for this technology to grow is huge. It can already deal with basic customer-facing scenarios. The clearest example of this so far is Hilton's adoption of an AI robot named 'Connie.' Customers who interact with the robot can get tourist information from it. Its ability to learn from human speech and adapt to individuals is particularly astounding. Finally, the more customers that interact with it, the better it will become Meet Connie, for example.

Chat bots and Messaging:

Front-facing customer service is perhaps the most obvious application of artificial intelligence in the hospitality industry. When it comes to direct messaging and online chat services, the technology has shown to be incredibly successful in responding to simple questions or requests. On social media platforms, for example, AI chat bots have been used to allow clients to ask questions and receive almost instantaneous responses, 24 hours a day, seven days a week. This is extremely beneficial to hotels since it allows them to achieve response times that are nearly difficult to achieve with human-to-human interaction.

Data Analysis:

Apart from customer service, data analysis is another area where AI is being used in the hotel business. The technology can be used in this capacity to sort through vast amounts of data fast and draw key conclusions about consumers or potential customers. The Dorchester Collection hotel chain, which uses the Metis AI platform as an example, is one such case. The company was able to go through data acquired via surveys, online reviews, and other means, and the AI was able to analyze it to derive judgments about overall performance.

More Digital Trends:

With digital technology advancing at a rapid pace, it's no wonder that its uses in the travel and hospitality business are growing as well. The most cutting-edge digital trends in the hospitality business are discussed in the following articles. The Hospitality Industry's Uses of Blockchain Technology. In the hospitality industry, there are eight examples of robots in use for facial Recognition, use Cases in the hospitality Industry. How to Turn a Hotel Room into a Smart Room in 7 Easy Steps.

Artificial Intelligence in healthcare:

People are clamoring for more sophisticated technologies to assist them or provide them with new perspectives or knowledge as technology advances. Artificial intelligence, or AI, is the intelligence demonstrated by computers or software, which is usually human-like intelligence. It has evolved into a discipline of research devoted to the development of intellect. Late John McCarthy of Stanford University originated the phrase "Artificial Intelligence" in 1956, and two years later, he presented his article, widely recognized as the first on logical AI. Alan Turing, a British mathematician, cryptanalyst, computer scientist, and biologist, created the Turing test to evaluate whether a machine can show intelligence. The test necessitates a human judge engaging in genuine discussions with both a human and a machine developed to mimic human performance. If the judge is unable to discern which of the two a human is and which is a machine, the machine is deemed intelligent.

Human Intelligence in Decision Making:

Human intellect is regarded as one of the most potent decision-making instruments. Human intelligence is defined as a person's ability to think like a human, which is characterized by perception, consciousness, self-awareness, and volition. Humans have the cognitive ability to learn, construct concepts, understand, apply logic, and reason because of their intellect. The talents to detect patterns, grasp ideas, plan, solve problems, make decisions, and retain and utilize language to communicate are also included. Decision making can be viewed as a cognitive methodology used to determine a conviction or a blueprint among a few options of possible outcomes. Intelligence allows humans to experience and think, whereas decision making can be viewed as a cognitive methodology used to determine a conviction or a blueprint among a few options of possible outcomes. Each decision-making mechanism generates a final choice that may or may not result in activity. The study of recognizing and selecting choices based on the chief's qualities and preferences is known as decision making. One of the most important aspects of administration is decision making, which is an integral part of any usage methodology.

Artificial Intelligence in Robotics:

Many industry observers have claimed that AI application is the most important and fascinating subject in robotic development. AI could be used in a variety of robots, including companion and caring robots, autonomous land, sea, and air vehicles, humanoid kinds, search and rescue robots, swarm robots, military robots, and robotic toys. Dexterous manipulation, autonomous navigation, machine vision, speech recognition, pattern recognition, and location and mapping are some of the AI elements that play a role . Humanoid robots and autonomous, mobile robots are the two robotic fields that have the most AI concepts. Honda's Asimo humanoid robot is the outcome of two decades of Honda engineers' research into humanoid robotics. Asimo can identify moving objects, gestures, postures, sounds, and faces, as well as interact with them in a human-like manner.

Artificial Intelligence in Healthcare:

Scientists have been tempted by advances in machine engineering to construct programming with the goal of assisting professionals in making decisions without consulting the authorities directly. Software development exploits human brainpower capabilities such as reasoning, decision-making, adaptation (through experience), and many others. Although artificial intelligence (AI) is not a new concept, it has been recognized as a source of software engineering innovation. It has been linked to a variety of fields, including education, business, medicine, and manufacturing. In most developing countries, a lack of medical professionals has increased patient mortality as a result of various infections. The lack of restorative professionals will never be remedied in a short period of time. Higher education institutions may, in such case, move quickly to deliver whatever numbers of specialists are necessary. However, many people may already be dying while waiting for understudies to become specialists and specialists to become experts. Patients were required to consult a master for further analysis and treatment under current practice for restorative treatment. Other therapy specialists may lack the necessary expertise or experience to handle certain high-risk illnesses.

Chapter 8: New Innovation on Healthcare and Hospitality

In a post-pandemic world, how are hospitals and health systems structuring their organizations for the future? While there are several ways in which innovation has expedited the change of healthcare delivery in the last year, here are six that stand out.

- AI stands for artificial intelligence.
- Cloud computing
- Virtual Intensive Care Unit
- Collaboration
- Tele health for inpatients via specially fitted in-room TVs
- Virtual Reality (VR) is a type of virtual

AI stands for artificial intelligence:

Artificial intelligence (AI) has enormous potential to revolutionize healthcare dynamics, but it is also one of the least understood technologies, due to misconceptions, promises, and legitimate worries. Regardless, AI is a fast-growing technological area, with Accenture predicting that it would reach $6.6 billion this year and that important clinical health AI applications may save the US healthcare system $150 billion annually by 2026.

Mayo Clinic and Google Take Relationship to Next Level:

Google, located in Mountain View, California, has announced that it will create a permanent office in Rochester, Minnesota, further cementing the burgeoning link between Mayo Clinic and Google. Improved radiation delivery systems, the creation of an AI factory, and the migration of 10 million patient records to the cloud have all come from collaboration to change patient care. "We've been hard at work creating the technological foundations for a lot of innovation, with security and privacy core to everything we do," said Cris Ross, MBA, Mayo Clinic's chief information officer, during a news conference on Thursday. "Having this new location to allow our cooperation will really help us accelerate innovation and work toward a common vision of a data-centric future, which we believe has the potential to improve patient, care, and provider experiences while also lowering healthcare costs."

5 Lessons Learned While Launching a Virtual ICU during the Pandemic:

In its effort to create a virtual ICU programmed for various hospitals in Allegheny Health Network (AHN), Pittsburgh-based Highmark Health not only increased its ability to care for critically sick patients, but it also laid the groundwork for future virtual care projects. "As we consider the larger spectrum of where virtual care may go," says Anil Singh, MD, MPH, MMM, executive medical director, enterprise clinical organization-clinical solutions, design, and implementation, Highmark Health. Highmark aims to collaborate with other local provider partners and AHN to implement similar tactics in local markets, while AHN will use this foundation to investigate future virtual projects.

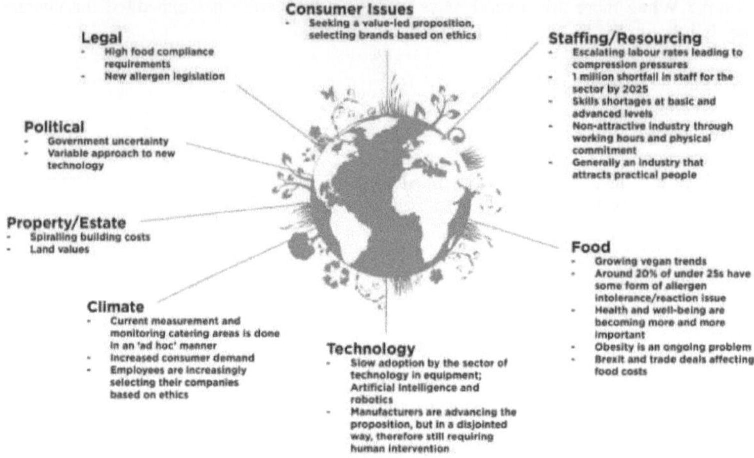

Figure No. 12 Innovative Technology System
Source: www.mya-consulting.co.uk/artificial-intelligence-the-robots-are-coming/

How Collaboration Accelerates Innovation during the Pandemic

The symbiotic link between health systems and the vendors that supply them has deepened throughout the epidemic, resulting in strong partnerships to adapt current products to meet emergent demands. Banner Health, located in Phoenix, runs 29 hospitals in six states, and Kyruus, based in Boston, have expanded their partnership to fulfill new COVID-19 testing and immunization schedule demands. "It's a virtuous cycle of constant improvement and innovations to repurpose current technology and apply them in more meaningful ways that genuinely alter your business," says Christen Castellano, vice president of Banner Health's customer experience channels.

Tele health TVs' Position Intermountain for the Future of Virtual Care:

Intermountain Healthcare has installed Amwell devices in patient rooms that turn smart televisions into tele health portals complete with a pan, tilt, and zoom camera and an unique microphone. The solution increases efficiency, improves cooperation, and prepares the health

system for the next phase of virtual care by allowing third parties to join the dialogue and allowing screen sharing.
"We're incorporating the infrastructure for telemedicine into all of our architectural plans," says Brian Wayling, MBA, Intermountain Healthcare's associate vice president of tele health services. Learn more about this breakthrough and its implications for healthcare in the future.

5 Ways Virtual Reality Can Better Prepare Future Surgeons:

With elective procedures suspended or postponed in recent months, the corona virus pandemic may have an unintended influence on the future of healthcare by postponing surgical resident training. To address this problem, the orthopedic surgery residency programmed at Marshall University Joan C. Edwards School of Medicine has implemented a virtual reality (VR) training curriculum. Marshall's current use of virtual reality highlights some of the inherent obstacles of surgical training, as well as how this expanding technology can educate a new generation of surgeons for the more sophisticated repertory of treatments they are now expected to execute. Another important feature of this programmed is that it provides new ways to "democratize" surgical training while both enhancing performance and speeding up the learning process

New Innovation on Hospitality Management:

 The term "innovation" refers to the act of introducing something new into the world. The goal of innovation is to provide better products and services to customers while also increasing organizational profits. "Innovation is new methods of performing the routine tasks, or unique or superior combinations of the production aspects," according to Hoteliers are doing research and development operations in order to offer unique products and services in order to attract clients and grow their businesses. In compared to chemical products, people prefer herbal products. Most individuals exclusively buy herbal and eco-friendly components in body care and food and beverage products, for example. In recent years, social activists, environmental authorities, and groups concerned about the environment have taken steps to pressure all industries to limit their processes that harm the environment. There are five primary aspects in the hotel sector where innovation occurs. Product and service innovation, process and logistics innovation, market and institutional innovation are all possibilities.

Product and service innovations: Strategic development in the field of product and service innovation is required for long-term success and a great bottom line. Process Innovations Hoteliers are developing new ways to provide services to their consumers. Customers are also considered for new roles in the unique service delivery process. Hotels are modernizing their work processes by implementing technology, such as automated front and back office services. The efficiency of the supply of services to customers has improved as a result of process innovation. Information Handling Process Innovations (Logistics Innovation): Organizational information flows are now becoming quicker. Due of the hectic schedules of guests, hoteliers are giving comprehensive information on the internet so that they may reserve a suite from a single window. Hoteliers are now in charge of managing supply chain relationships with travel agencies, courier services, and tourism in order to make things easier for guests. Market

Innovations: Promotional efforts are crucial for every business. Hoteliers are now using new ways of communication to interact with their consumers. Influencing elements of innovation in Hotel industry

In The Hotel, There Are Five Factors That Influence Innovation.

Innovation supporting process, radical innovation necessitates thorough strategic planning, as well as sufficient funds and capital. To inspire employees, a well-developed employee assessment and pay strategy should be in place. Knowledge management, as well as training and development, are essential to motivate every employee in the company to contribute to the company's business plan. Firm (Hotel) Size. The size of the company has a significant impact on the innovation process. If a company is large and operates internationally, it will take a different strategy. Supplier Driven, hotels are a supply-driven industry that aims for standardized products in order to maximize profit. The hotel's reputable suppliers provide value for it.

Market Factor and Competition

Firms must establish a well-developed marketing plan in order to compete effectively. The primary factors that a hotelier should focus on for strategically developing market efforts include building guest loyalty, giving higher customer pleasure, connecting with customer emotions, earning the high value of visitor experience, and embracing newest trends in the hotel. The way a hotelier treats a visitor is really significant. The hotel's particular attention to guests always leaves them satisfied. However, it varies from person to person. For example, children prefer gadgets over one-on-one attention and urge that their parents accompany them to such a location. Loyalty programmers provide a wonderful chance for customization by allowing you to invite a larger number of consumers. Corporate programmers are designed to not only treat visitors as individuals, but also to interact with their most important clients, allowing them to take advantage of additional chances.

"Give me an experience," a guest has always anticipated from a hotel. Guests looking for extra activities when visiting a new location. Customers are looking for unexpected experiences that go beyond their ideas and sentiments and engage their senses. Hoteliers should focus more on how to connect with emotions in their customer loyalty programmed than on rational, incentive-based offerings. Customers usually travel on vacation and prefer hotel services. Essentially, activity-based travel provides rich emotional experiences that hoteliers may advertise to attract clients. Various activity-based travel trends are now gaining popularity in the industry. It might be a cultural club, because many people nowadays choose to attend to the theatre, visit historic places, or participate in educational activities while on vacation. Customers' spending power is growing in tandem with the economy, and as a result, they are willing to pay more for higher-quality items. Adventure tourism is another trend in activity-based travel. The major goal of this activity-based vacation is to keep fit and healthy by visiting famous parks, hiking, and engaging in other adventurous activities.

With this in mind, resorts are increasingly providing guests with simple automobiles at a low cost or for free to explore the local area. Heritage tourism is also used to commemorate any well-known location, community, or historical site.

People's attitudes on pricing have shifted, and as the economy has risen and fallen, they are becoming more concerned about the goods and quality for which they are paying. As a result, individuals are weighing the value of what they are receiving vs. what they are spending. However, the most pressing challenge for hoteliers is to enhance value at the same price, which necessitated product, process, logistics, marketing communication, and institutional innovation. There are generally five things that

Provide Value To A Customer's Stay At A Hotel, As Listed Below:

An hotelier might innovate in terms of room size and comfort level in the guest room design. The hotel's staff should pay close attention to the cleanliness of the guests' rooms and other moving spaces. The guest's room should be adorned with traditional furnishings. The lighting system drapes, and entertainment layout should all be tailored to the guest's preferences. Physical property: A hotel's interior and outside architecture contribute to its worth. Interpersonal Service: Hotel employees must demonstrate service friendliness and special attention to potential consumers. The professionalism and personal recognition shown by personnel is always appreciated by the guests. These characteristics bring a grin to the guest's face and encourage favorable word-of-mouth about the hotel. Functional Services: Employees of any hotel or company are expected to be efficient and provide prompt service.

Food and Beverage-Related Service:

This is the most crucial element that guests recall when describing their hotel experience. Food and beverage are the enjoyable and sociable aspects of a customer's visit. The role of Employees in Innovation every company must encourage and reward innovation and originality among its personnel. This necessitated a compromise between the pressing needs to improve efficiency, quality, and production. Employees generate new ideas and concepts, or new connections between existing ideas and concepts, in this complicated and chaotic creative process. Teresa Amiable (1998) asserts, "Every individual's creativity is a product of three factors: expertise, innovative thinking, and motivation." Expertise is a result of experience. Employees participate in a function over time and get in-depth expertise in that sector. This information is acquired not just via formal schooling, but also through on-the-job experience and interactions with other professionals. Every company today encourages employees to share their expertise and knowledge through a knowledge sharing programmed (KSP). By engaging in these types of activities, you are cultivating an intellectual space in which you may examine obstacles and problems. Employees become more active and conscious of the need to solve challenges.

Practices lead to creative thinking. It is a skillful and determined cognitive process that determines an individual's adaptability and innovative capacity to solve an issue. It provides a person a lot of room to think beyond the box. Firms are now encouraging workers to bring fresh perspectives to reality, to combine existing ideas in novel ways, to flip problems on their heads, and to enable unexpected paths and ideas from other sectors. The personality of a person, as well as his or her way of thinking and functioning, had a significant impact on his or her ability to think creatively.

The individual is motivated to perform things after receiving input from the aforementioned two elements. Expertise and innovative ideas are useless if there is a lack of motivation. A motivated worker may accomplish a task more effectively and creatively.

The hotel sector is currently fostering innovation and ideas in conjunction with these three characteristics. Firms occasionally organize training programmers for workers in brainstorming, problem solving, and lateral thinking skills, which can improve employees' talents and hence add to productivity.

- Problem-Solving
- Brainstorming
- Thinking in Different Ways

The firm's dedication to learning is taken into account when determining its capability for innovation and creativity. If employees get advanced expertise in their industries, it will undoubtedly benefit company chances. To avoid any strange occurrences, employees will become more aware and responsible. Employees benefit from training programmers because they update and revitalize their knowledge and provide access to the outside world. A company learns through providing learning opportunities to each of its employees, and it benefits from their efforts. The sharing of relevant information among colleagues in a group contributes to organizational growth. Employees benefit a company even if it absorbs superior methods, procedures, advanced technology, personnel, and competences from other companies. The most important thing is that the employee has a learning mentality that can help the company succeed. Giving money as an incentive is ineffective in motivating personnel.

Extrinsic and intrinsic successes should be included in the rewards system. There are numerous more methods to motivate employees besides using a reward tool as an added incentive. Human resource management is now accorded equal weight in terms of contributing to corporate success. They come up with innovative ideas to keep the employee motivated. Employees are encouraged to offer their thoughts, innovative ideas, and unique solutions to issues to regular job tasks, and one of the incentive systems is a sense of success.

Hospitality Trends (Eco-Friendly Initiatives):

The worldwide hotel business is primarily grappling with the issue of decreasing occupancy rates. Hoteliers, like any other sector, are placing a greater emphasis on originality and innovation in order to attract consumers and gain loyalty. Inevitably, luxury facilities are given high attention in the healthcare sector, and at a fair cost. To provide a luxury facility, hotels must work 24 hours a day, seven days a week to differentiate themselves in terms of the originality and degree of comfort they deliver to customers, as well as justifying the higher costs. The hotel industry is divided into segments based on the services provided, such as.

Hotels with a Personal Touch:'

The traditional participants in the hospitality industry are boutique hotels. The tagline for the hotel sector right now is "Change the Times." To substitute the monotonous performances, boutique hotels mostly provide late-night dance clubs and techno grooves.

Spa Energy:

The industry of "energy medicine" is expanding at a quicker rate. This can be classified as a part of the hospitality industry. People in the business sector are working hard to stay afloat in the face of intense competition. People's health is deteriorating as a result of their stressful schedules. They choose to go to hotels for energy-spa treatments to help them balance their body, mind, and soul. This is a highly sought-after stress-reduction therapy. Mini treatments, such as five-minute massages, are quite fashionable these days. During their stay at the hotel, hoteliers provide spa services to customers in order to change their exhausted energy into active and lively energy. This is popular not just among working people, but also among the elderly who prefer this type of treatment.

There aren't any pet-friendly initiatives:

Many hotels do not allow dogs because certain clients do not like them. Pets are no longer permitted on the red carpet that has been laid out for the attendees. In most cases, pets lie on guest beds and move into other visitors' areas, causing problems for them as well. Because of the pet, hotel employees must make extra steps to change the bed sheets and pillow covers, as well as properly launder them.

Traditional Wines are making a Comeback:

Some of the hotel's appealing guests serve in the restaurant because they don't want to compromise on the quality or flavor of the wines.

Eco-Friendly Hospitality Initiatives

As previously said, every business is currently taking steps to become more environmentally friendly. There is a trend in the hotel industry to become environmentally friendly for good reasons, and this initiative helps them market themselves. On a daily basis, the hotel's operational procedures, such as cooking, power and water consumption, have an impact on the environment. The hotel business has also begun to advocate for environmental sustainability and considerable energy reduction. Because they are built amid rainforests, eco-friendly hotels are initially considered as being located in a very nature-focused environment. The industry encourages consumers to reduce their carbon impact and obtain a green label. Environmental training programmers are now available for hotel personnel to help them become more environmentally conscious. Hotels seek to construct their buildings using only environmentally friendly, long-lasting materials. It's difficult for them to find sources for these raw materials, such as local stone and tropical hardwood. However, environmentally concerned hotels are making every effort to establish a specific green ideology. It is not just the business owner who is actively promoting the conversion to a green mentality, but also the government. Guests are taught to recycle at home and choose to drive a more environmentally friendly vehicle to conserve electricity. Hoteliers are always attempting to demonstrate best practices to their visitors. The following are a few green best practices features.

Hotels That Are Environmentally Friendly Are In Tune With Nature:

Customers may enjoy a harmonious atmosphere in environmentally friendly hotels. It is generally placed in a calm environment with well-managed eco-friendly techniques such as rainwater recycling. The hotels' dedication to become environmentally friendly and their appreciation for nature is seen in every tiny activity.

'Green' Hotels That Rule The Roost Benefit The Environment In The Following Ways:

The greatest amenities that help the environment are found in really green hotels. The hotels urge its guests to enjoy the natural beauty of the surroundings. This allows people to spend precious time connecting with nature and appreciating the experience. Guests may contribute to the preservation of natural resources by appreciating and understanding the environment. Green hotels provide a unique atmosphere that provides actual comfort and more than simply a good night's sleep. Because of the natural surroundings, visitors' minds are compelled to think about the environment and to take the required steps to help in this direction.

Eco-Friendly Lodging Helps To Reduce Material Use.

It is true that eco-friendly lodging aids in the reduction of material usage. It's one of the most appealing characteristics of real green status, and it's also one of the simplest to achieve. Green hotels are really devoted to becoming ecologically friendly, and they make substantial efforts to reduce their hotel's material use. Rainfall harvesting to recycle rainwater, waste recycling, and the usage of environmentally friendly items demonstrate the hotels' concern for the environment.

A Proactive Environmental Strategy Should Be Implemented By An Eco Hotel:

Green hotels have proactive environmental policies that are easily adopted by both visitors and hotel personnel. Genuine green hotels have formed their own environmental policy and urge their workers and visitors to adopt it. Hotel employees are required to get training in order to instil green thinking in as many ways as possible, according to regulation.

Luxury and accommodation comfort are not sacrificed in an eco-friendly hotel:

There is no need for an enlightened green hotel to forego comfort and luxury in the name of sustainability. In the luxury hotel, comfortable beds are supplied for resting while also benefiting the environment through active sheet re-use programmers, utilizing rain water for toilet flushing in the luxury bathroom, and towel re-use schemes that reduce laundry. For the decorating of the guest room, the hotel's management always chooses healthy green furnishings and cleaning materials, and the flooring are also designed to create a natural consciousness.

Green habits are easy to incorporate into daily life, and some aren't even necessary for certification. For example, no certification is necessary for the use of non-toxic cleaning solutions such as laundry detergent, dishwashing liquids, and other hotel supplies. New technologies, such as solar and wind energy, are now on the horizon to partially replace electrical energy. Although it necessitates adequate infrastructure for installation, it significantly reduces electricity consumption. As a result, hotels should use this type of technology to conserve energy.

- Cavendish Hotel

The Cavendish, a magnificent Jermyn Street hotel in downtown London, is noted for its eco-pioneering. Cavendish Hotel is the most environmentally aware hotel in London, having won the most prestigious honor, the Green Tourism for London gold medal. In addition, it has received a slew of other awards for its efforts. The Cavendish has a very ecologically friendly workplace culture that can be observed through every pore. Hotel Cavendish, for example, purchases ethically produced coffee and fair trade tea for its guests. Only eco-friendly chemicals are used throughout, and suppliers are carefully consulted to decrease packing and transit time. Its waste products are recycled on a regular basis. It has received Gold Award in Sustainable Tourism, 3-Star Accreditation by the SRA (Sustainable Restaurant Association), and the Icarus Environmental Award for its altruistic activities.

- Park Plaza Hotel

This hotel has formed collaboration with a carbon-neutral firm to carry out worldwide carbon-reduction programmers in order to reduce the hotel's environmental effect.
The Strand Palace Hotel is a luxury hotel in London.
To save energy, Property Strand Palace has installed low-energy lighting bulbs throughout the hotel. The hotel prefers to utilize biodegradable and environmentally friendly chemicals. It generates electricity by combining the functioning of heating and power units, reducing CO2 emissions. To deal with environmental challenges, the Hotel Strand Palace has hired a specialized Green team.

Chapter 9: Economic Growth in Healthcare

For decades, the cost of health care has been increasing in the United States' economy. This has drawn a lot of attention to the problem and the source of the spending increase. Population demographics, medical technological developments, price inflation, and changes in health care consumption were found as contributing variables after a thorough review. The economy of the United States and health-care spending are inextricably linked. Experts believe that unless steps are made to slow this surge, economic development and jobs would suffer as a result.

What Impact Does Health Care Have on the Economy?

According to a poll of CEOs in the United States, the majority of company executives are concerned about the expense of employee health care. The impact of increased healthcare expenses on the government budget is likewise problematic.

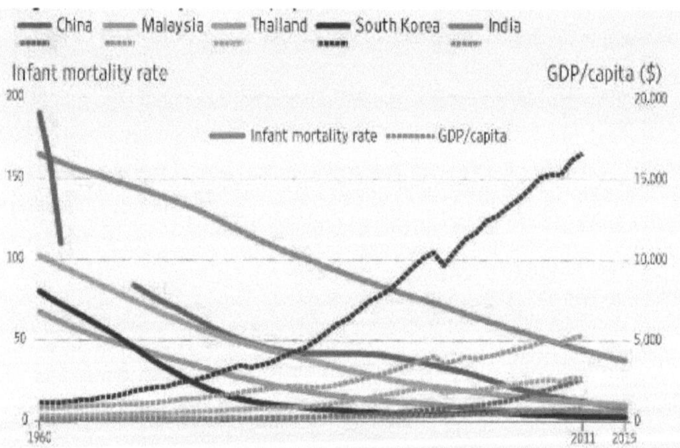

Figure No. 13 Economic Growth Metrics
Source: https://www.livemint.com/Politics/PuYLifV8TNzD13GqiK3JmN/Healthcare-and-economic-growth.html

When it comes to health care, it's not all doom and gloom; some economists see this as a positive indication. When measured in terms of quality, health-care costs are falling, and more individuals are gaining access to modern medical technologies. At the municipal level, growing health-care costs are advantageous since they result in more jobs for people, higher wages for healthcare workers, and more tax revenue.

The Economic Impact on Health Care

By now, it should be obvious that health care and the US economy are inextricably interwoven. Health care is sometimes even referred to as the economy. It employs a vast number of people, and the following are some of the economic health-care implications.

- **Reduced Funding -** Any private hospital's principal goal is to maximize profits and satisfy its owners. This has a negative impact on the hospital's personnel, patients, and the broader public. There is a scarcity of finances from all sources, including the government, the public sector, and the private sector.

- **More Uninsured Families** — Since a result of the increase in unemployment, the number of uninsured families has risen, as many families have lost their employer-sponsored insurance. Many of these families are unable to keep their own insurance coverage. Hospitals and insurance companies are in business to earn money, thus they would not cover a pre-existing condition. As a result, the youngsters are more susceptible to disease. And as the unemployment rate rises, the problem is just going to grow worse.

- **Obesity Rate Increases -** Despite the fact that we have never been more knowledgeable about obesity, the rate of obesity continues to rise. In the United States, it is believed that one out of every three children is fat. Obesity is linked to a number of disorders, including diabetes, high cholesterol, high blood pressure, heart attack, stroke, and cancer. The health-care system is severely strained as a result.

- **Staff Shortage -** Due to a lack of funds, physicians and nurses are in limited supply, and those who are available are forced to work overtime, exhausting themselves and lowering the quality of patient treatment. This can be disastrous since the physicians do not have enough time to conduct a thorough examination. Hundreds of people die each year as a result of this, yet hospitals remain oblivious to it.

- **Pharmaceutical Company Control** – The cost of drugs is the ultimate economic problem impacting healthcare. Pharmaceutical corporations are responsible for developing new treatments for chronic diseases, but they have become greedy and are raising medicine prices, making them unavailable to individuals with little financial resources.

According to a 2003 survey, overall health-care spending increased to $1.7 trillion, or $5670 per person. In 1960, national health expenditures were $27 billion; by 1985, they had risen to $427 billion, or 10.1 percent of GDP, in slightly over two and a half decades. In another two decades, it will have surpassed $2 trillion, significantly exceeding the GDP of most countries. By 2013, national health expenditures are predicted to reach $3.4 trillion, accounting for 18.4 percent of GDP.

Chapter 10: Economic growth in hospitality

The hotel business is fast expanding and already accounts for about 10% of global GDP in recent decades, the hotel business has placed a high value on a rapid expansion process. As a result, the hotel business is expanding internationally and fostering growth in a rapidly changing multicultural environment. At the regional, national, and global levels, hospitality is being developed. Locally and regionally, an internationally oriented hospitality industry with many enterprises competes, a slew of data point to the International Monetary Fund's forecast of economic growth, which would be unevenly split between developing countries (6.4 percent) and industrialized nations (2.2 percent). The hospitality business has various subsectors, with hotels and restaurants being one of the most important sources of economic growth.

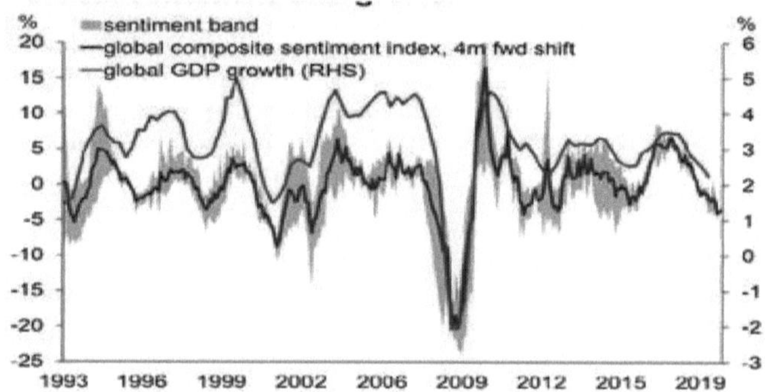

Figure No. 14 Economic Growth in Hospitality
Source: https://www.rev-mantra.com/post/a-perfect-storm-impact-of-economic-slowdown-trade-wars-and-convid-19-on-asian-hospitality-industry

Tourism and hospitality are two phrases that are sometimes used interchangeably and are lumped together as a single business. However, the hospitality and tourist industries are seen as two distinct enterprises. There is a lot of overlap between these two. Tourism is defined as people travelling and visiting areas outside of their typical surroundings for less than a year for business or pleasure; they are not working there while visiting places.

Hospitality refers to the provision of lodging, venues, meals, and beverages to persons who are away from their homes. The people of the United Kingdom, as well as other non-resident residents, benefit from these services. Restaurants, lodging, hotels, and other exposition activities are all covered by both of these businesses. Tourism is not just a source of tourist services; it is a subsector of hospitality. We have drawn a clear distinction between two overlapping industries in this way (www.baha-uk.org). We go on with our topic to finish the duty of hospitality and its subsectors.

- Clubs with a license
- Shops selling food
- Catering services
- Catering services provided on-site
- Activities of exhibition and fair organizers
- Conference organizer's activities
- Other types of food services

These are segments of the hotel business that offer services in a variety of ways. In nations where tourism is a key export business, hospitality is a main point. The hospitality industry has benefited from the cross-border migration of businesspeople and capital. The hotel industry is the primary source of foreign currency exchange and one of the major employments in the country. Hospitality draws people from all walks of life together in a global community. Countries with negative trade balances are looking to hospitality and tourism to help them close the gap. As a result, hospitality is more than a concept; it is a driving force in the global marketplace. Lifestyle and commercial globalization are conveyed in other languages while dealing with various political and social systems. To thrive, hospitality businesses must think worldwide, and rival hospitality businesses in the United Kingdom and the United States are mature. Companies competing in all facets of the hotel business will expand their operations outside their borders. The notion that global entities with advantages will compete in the future as a result of globalization is unacceptably naive.

Hotels are categorized based on season and services, such as the difference between a Motel 6 and a four-season hotel. The Marriott Corporation is a well-known brand that caters to a wide range of pricing and service levels, as well as the extended stay and luxury holiday segments. Resorts and Suites at Marriot Hotels

- Marriot's Courtyard
- Marriot Spring Hill suits
- Conference Centers by Marriott
- International Marriot Vacation Club
- Marriot Residence Inn

As A Market Category, Marriot Runs and Owns A Luxury Hotel Group:

Next WWII, hotel chains flourished rapidly, especially in the following two decades. The pressure of expanding hotel enterprises is driving the tendency to expand outside national borders. These businesses are racing to the key point where their land is adequate to please tourists and meet their demands. The hotel sub-sector of hospitality may reach a stage where the consumer has no other choice. The hotel market in America, as well as its leadership, may draw attention to the possibility of expanding into Asia/Pacific markets to compete with regional enterprises. Customers are introduced to worldwide brands and goods by these global hospitality firms. In the worldwide market, a large number of hotels have built single brands and goods in a highly identical manner. Tourists and visitors are also in demand for distinctive local items from the hotel business, according to research. As a result, worldwide corporations have attempted to represent local design in some way.

The Hospitality Sector (Hotels And Restaurants) Is Critical To The Industry's Success:

Hotel projects are critical for creating new job opportunities and stimulating local economies. In general, hotels offer two sorts of services: I lodging and (ii) eating services. Foreign visitors, domestic households, and institutional purchases are among the industry's customers. The major three elements that influence the accommodation facilities and hotel choices are competitive price, availability of services, and the level of complimentary services. The number of visitors has increased at a 9% yearly pace during the last five years. For more than half of all international travelers, hotels are the primary and most popular form of lodging.

Hotels and Hospitality:

We'd want to learn more about the many sorts of businesses that major resort hotels cover. Hotel provision is under the umbrella of hospitality, which encompasses a wide range of services that include shelter and personal amenities. Hotels and other establishments catered to folks who travel for both personal and professional reasons. At the worldwide level, it has been estimated that almost 700 million tourists have arrived. This data reveals a 241.5 million rise in the previous 10 years, with a 4.9 percent annual growth rate. Europe was the most significant area for tourist arrivals, with a 4.5 percent yearly change in market growth, after the Middle East (10.7 percent), Eastern Asia and Africa (6.6 percent), and Western Asia (8.8%). The availability of finance is a critical factor in the growth of hotels and hotel enterprises. Personal assistance, loans, investment corporations, stocks and shares, and governments are the primary sources of funding for hotel growth.

Employment and Hospitality:

More than 2.5 million individuals in the UK are employed in the hospitality industry, which employs more than 10% of the workforce. There are two primary categories in the hotel industry. The hospitality industry (clubs, bars, restaurants, hotels, and contract catering) made over two-thirds of the total. Second, one-third of the industry is made up of hospitality services such as restaurants and hospitals. This area of the hospitality industry employs both full-time and part-time workers. It should be mentioned that employment is contingent on industry working circumstances such as weekends, long hours, and other flexibility.

- Catering
- Restaurant
- Accommodation
- Hotels

- Transport
- Attractions for visitors
- Consumer
- Recreational opportunities
- Government
- Intermediaries
- Services Not Listed

Industrial sector of leisure and Hospitality:

The leisure industry's key components and consumers, such as visitors or travelers, are the industry's focus point. Hundreds of leisure items are developed by companies of all sizes on the international market. These organizations work in the public and private sectors both locally and abroad. Large leisure product providers are aware of their target clients and consider their needs across national borders. Global fast food chains are now common in Europe market for the global fast food chains. Due to development and openness of this growth in world has made rapid growth in their economies. The rapid growth of franchised fast foods at the McDonalds, Burger King and Pizza Hut have invited the youth of America and all around the world to see the culture. Hospitality industry keeps the hotel business with different products, methods, and technology and less easy to analyze it. Hotel industry produces many products in varying sale markets of the world. It keeps close contacts with its customers who consume the products at the sale points.

Reference:

1. Berry, L. L., & Mirabito, A. M. (2010). Innovative healthcare delivery. *Business Horizons, 53*(2), 157-169.

2. Cooper, R. G., & Mohabeersingh, C. (2008). Lean thinking in a healthcare system-innovative roles. *Journal of Pre-Clinical and Clinical Research, 2*(2).

3. Shah, M. N., Gillespie, S. M., Wood, N., Wasserman, E. B., Nelson, D. L., Dozier, A., & McConnochie, K. M. (2013). High-intensity telemedicine-enhanced acute care for older adults: an innovative healthcare delivery model. *Journal of the American Geriatrics Society, 61*(11), 2000-2007.

4. Kaba, A., & Barnes, S. (2019). Commissioning simulations to test new healthcare facilities: a proactive and innovative approach to healthcare system safety. *Advances in Simulation, 4*(1), 1-9.

5. Ariani, A., Koesoema, A. P., & Soegijoko, S. (2017). Innovative healthcare applications of ICT for developing countries. In *Innovative Healthcare Systems for the 21st Century* (pp. 15-70). Springer, Cham.

6. Mottaeva, A., & Zheltenkov, A. (2018). Innovative capacity as a factor of the municipal healthcare system development. In *MATEC Web of Conferences* (Vol. 170, p. 01022). EDP Sciences.

7. Bashkin, O., Dopelt, K., Asna, N., & Davidovitch, N. (2021). Recommending Unfunded Innovative Cancer Therapies: Ethical vs. Clinical Perspectives among Oncologists on a Public Healthcare System—A Mixed-Methods Study. *Current Oncology, 28*(4), 2902-2913.

8. Yeh, K. H. (2016). A secure IoT-based healthcare system with body sensor networks. *IEEE Access, 4*, 10288-10299.

9. Kuo, C. M., Chen, L. C., & Tseng, C. Y. (2017). Investigating an innovative service with hospitality robots. *International Journal of Contemporary Hospitality Management.*

10. Elfimova, Y., & Radishauskas, T. (2018). Management of innovative activity in the field of hospitality. In *Sustainable development of tourism market: international practices and Russian experience* (pp. 57-59).

11. Morozov, M., & Morozova, N. (2019, October). Innovative staff training strategies for the tourism and hospitality industry. In *5th International Conference on Economics, Management, Law and Education (EMLE 2019)* (pp. 393-396). Atlantis Press.

12. Dzhandzhugazova, E. A., Blinova, E. A., Orlova, L. N., & Romanova, M. M. (2016). Innovations in hospitality industry. *International Journal of Environmental and Science Education, 11*(17), 10387-10400.

13. Gelbman, A. (2021). Tourist Experience and Innovative Hospitality Management in Different Cities. *Sustainability, 13*(12), 6578.

14. Dahiya, A. (2013). Hospitality and Tourism Education in India: In Search of Innovative Programmes. *Productivity*, *53*(4).

15. Zeveke, O. (2015). Innovative instruments of internet marketing in hospitality sphere. In *Social and economic innovations: trends, forecasts and perspectives* (pp. 108-111).

Printed by Books on Demand GmbH, Norderstedt / Germany